Mythological Beings From Portugal

(Edition 1.2)

Miguel Carvalho Abrantes

When I wrote my previous book, *Famous Legends from Portugal*, I was unaware if English-speaking people had any real interest in the subject at hand. Soon after, I was made aware that some readers appeared to have liked it, which eventually led me to the idea of creating a follow up of some sort. However, at first I was unsure on what topic to cover in it, since jumping straight away to a work retelling 3000+ regional legends from this country seemed like a very daunting and imprudent task.

Then, one day, as I was hiking in the forests of *Sintra*[1], I came across the mysterious *Anta de Adrenunes* and jokingly commented with a friend that such a place would be the perfect location to find a *Moura Encantada*. She was unaware of such mythological being – formerly one of the most famous in this country – and I quickly told her a story about it. The next few days I tried asking other people about this and other similar beings from our country, but with the exclusion of the most famous ones (such as the *Bruxa* or the *Lobisomem*), which they apparently only knew through the popular culture of Europe and North America, they appeared to be mostly unaware of Portugal's own native mythological beings. Even worse – sometimes, they would unlock their phones to try to look them up online, and ended up either finding very incomplete information, or wholly unreliable one, which appeared to be completely made up. Such a problem was what eventually led me to the idea of compiling this new book, about mythological beings native to Portugal, with the intention of trying to save them from the complete forgetfulness of a time where everyone seems to know the

---

1   All Portuguese text contained in this book is presented *in italic*. They are generally names of places or beings, but when necessary they are followed by an English translation.

"Werewolf", but are unaware of our native *Lobisomem* and its unique characteristics.

In order to compile a reliable work on this subject I knew I had to bring out some big guns. When the famous Brothers Grimm published their research on popular oral tales from Germany, this soon led to many other countries from Europe compiling their own local stories and figures. Naturally, such compilation also took place in Portugal, and so I knew that was a great point to start my research. As part of the study for my own *Sources of Myths, Legends and Classical Literature*[2], I was already aware of certain literary sources that, although only available in Portuguese, would be very helpful in this search – Adolfo Coelho's *Obra Etnográfica I*; Consiglieri Pedroso's *Contribuições para uma Mitologia Popular Portuguesa e Outros Escritos Etnográficos*; Leite de Vasconcellos' *Anuário para o Estudo das Tradições Populares Portuguezas* and *Tradições Populares de Portugal*; Teófilo Braga's *O Povo Portuguez nos seus Costumes, Crenças e Tradições*; and two magazines, *A Tradição* and *Revista Lusitana*; among other less known sources. Starting from those, I compiled all references to mythological creatures natively associated with Portugal, and then quickly defined that what I sought, specifically, were fantastic beings, ones which had some kind of unusual characteristic impossible to normal humans or animals.

Then, I compared the information I had collected with two different websites, Mitologia.pt and Lendarium.org[3],

---

2   That book is constantly being updated across time and can be obtained for free on Archive.org .

3   Although this second website contains a very large number of Portuguese stories and legends, it should also be noted that it is very frequently down.

hoping to find even more creatures, or at least some additional elements which could reveal more information about each creature I knew of.

Finally, I asked native (and older) people about some of these figures and their potential legends. Although two of the many people I interviewed proved specially useful, they could only recall a very limited number of these beings, and almost always as very faint memories from their youth[4] – and yet, their information made it possible to add a few more elements to this work, ones that were apparently never before preserved in a written form.

Having obtained all that information, I subsequently synthesized it for this book, essentially trying to find out which beings simply had different names in different areas of the country (e.g. the *Medo* and the *Trango-Mango*), and how their unique characteristics could be described in order to give readers the most extensive information possible for each of them. But, in spite of that effort, this still has to be a book of incompleteness – some creatures native to Portugal, like the *Homem das Sete Dentaduras* or the *Tatro Azeiteiro*, are now almost completely forgotten, and so, all across this book, you will be able to read about some creatures that may raise a thousand questions in your head, but for which very few answers are currently available. It is not for any lack of research that they are presented like that, but exclusively because they were already partially lost when their stories were first collected at the end of the XIX century and, ultimately, it proved impossible to save them until our XXI century. Even other books which attempted a similar task in

So, if you ever want to use it, you may have to try multiple times during different days in order to be able to do so.

4   It should certainly be noted they were over 80 years old now.

recent years, such as Nuno Matos Valente's *Bestiário Tradicional Português*, present them as they're also shown here – sadly incomplete, tantalizing, raising more questions than we're now able to answer.

In spite of that unavoidable problem, I truly hope that the information collected here, and here also presented for the very first time in the English language, can somehow contribute to save creatures such as the *Tardo*, the *Maria Gancha* or the *Velha da Égua Branca* from complete forgetfulness, through their presentation to an international audience which certainly never heard about them before. That is, perhaps most of all, the ultimate goal of this new book – by presenting these beings to everyone who speaks English, maybe one day they will be as known across the world as the Irish "Kelpie" or the American "Sasquatch", and perhaps their stories will live forever.

I truly hope you enjoy this book, at least as much as I had my pleasure in collecting all this information, while learning more and more about these beings and trying to present them an English-speaking audience.

Miguel Carvalho Abrantes

P.S.- This work is dedicated to *Bé*, *Dona Conceição* and everyone who inspired me in this search for now-almost-forgotten beings native to the country of Portugal.

Index

1. *Alicórnio*
Translation: "Alicorn"[5]

In the context of Portuguese Mythology, the *Alicórnio* was a giant with a single eye in the middle of his forehead. I was only able to find a reference to it in a single fictional story, one very similar to the episode of Polyphemus in Homer's *Odyssey*. Given the fact that a very similar story is also associated with another similar creature, the *Olharapo*, chances are that this kind of being simply received different names in different locations, and that the Portuguese people once had many local designations for what is now known as a Cyclops.

2. *Alma de Mestre*
Translation: "Soul of a Master"

When Portuguese sailors traveled all over the world, they would frequently find unusual birds flying over their ships. This apparently led them to the idea that some of those creatures – the identity of the actual bird(s) involved in this belief is now hard to establish – were not merely flying animals, but a temporary reincarnation of some notable sailor, such as a captain or the master of a ship, who had somehow become lost at sea and now tried to prevent a similar fate for those who shared his profession. Supposedly, this kind of "curse" would remain in effect until their human

---

5   For each being I tried to provide an approximate English translation of the original's meaning. If you see it is under quotation marks it means it's an approximation, but if you see it without them it means that the name provided captures very well the original's.

body was finally taken to a shore and given a christian
burial, at which point the soul would finally get its deserved
rest.

3. *Alma Penada*
Translation: "Soul in Torment"
Also Known As: *Abusões, Almas do Outro Mundo, Avejãs*
   (or *Avejões*, in their male form), *Aventesma, Bisarma,*
   Fantasma, Fogachos, Fogos Fátuos[6]

When I first started compiling information for this
book, I quickly noticed that many creatures from Portuguese
Mythology were almost entirely lost. However, there are also
a very limited number which once were, and still continue to
be, significantly famous. This class of beings are certainly
among them, but a problem quickly arises when trying to
report their story – although they go by many names, and
some even have very unique abilities (e.g. the *Bisarma* was a
giant-like ghost), they seem to share some significant
characteristics, which certainly proves they were known by
different names in different places, instead of being
completely different creatures.

Beginning with their most famous name, an *Alma
Penada* is, literally translated, a soul of a dead person which
is still suffering some kind of penalty. Popular tradition
seems to preserve at least two reasons for such a heinous fate
– they were either people who made a promise to God or the
saints and ended up not fulfilling it, or they were farmers
who evilly messed around with the limits of their own

---

6   When the same creature was apparently known under many different
     names, I tried to present them in association with their most famous one, as
     you can first see here.

terrains[7]. In both cases, when the person died their soul was convicted to roam the earth until someone was kind enough to help them. Their descriptions, under such adventures, vary a bit, but they were often imagined as a kind of white ghosts, either regular size or gigantic, who cried and lamented their current fate.

Although in some cases you could prevent such transformations from ever taking place by removing all the water from the house before the person died – remember, this was way before houses had running water, and so getting more of it was frequently a hard task – that is an element that seems to have been lost across the decades. However, what is certainly more interesting and worthy of note is the fact that some people, usually older ones, still occasionally believe in the existence of this class of beings. I was reported three different stories, which deserve to be preserved here:

A first reporter, a woman in her 80s who originally lived near Viseu, told me that when she was a young girl, strange noises could be heard near her house during the night. Her neighbors heard them too. Some people assumed those were *Almas Penadas*, others thought they were *Lobisomens*, but it was eventually found out that they were simply the young bakers of the village running to get to their work place in the middle of the night. Unfortunately, I was not further explained how this was found out, instead being repeatedly told she now knew it all to be just pure fantasies and nothing else.

---

7   In Portugal, traditionally the limits of terrains were marked through specific landmarks. Although some of them were naturally hard to move, such as a tree or a well, others, such as stones, could have their location changed without much difficulty.

4

A second reporter, an 85 year old woman whose family came from the north of Portugal, shared two stories about these beings, both of which had occurred with her. In the first one, back when she was just a young child, she used to hear strange noises, similar to weavers working and falling needles, over the ceiling of her house, something which was particularly weird given the fact the house had a single floor. In some undisclosed way, it was later found out that a seamstress had lived there and had promised a dress to an image of the Virgin Mary, but had died before being able to offer one; and so, when the promise was eventually fulfilled by the living, the whole occurrence quickly ceased. Following from this context, it should be noted that although this woman insisted this had truly and undeniably happened to her, other similar stories were once reported all over Portugal (and even internationally). As such, it is possible this was just a story she heard from her family, many decades ago, and which ended up scaring her so much that she later assumed it had literally happened to her.

However, she also reported another story, one which her own husband also presented as being true and having happened to them. Many years before, when they were living near *Bragança*, their leisure nights would occasionally be interrupted by loud bangs in their front door. They, and their friends, were very scared by this, but eventually her husband decided to shout *"Diga ao que vem!"*[8] This prompted an unknown and unrecognizable voice to request some produce, something alone the lines of "I need one kilogram of rice"[9]. They obtained it the next day, left it outside, and the loud bangs weren't heard ever again.

8   I.e. "Tell me what you seek!" This same expression also appears in this exact same context in many other stories associated with *Almas Penadas*.

Perhaps it also deserves to be noted that, although in stories and reports people are usually more than glad to cater to the requests (seemingly) made by this class of beings, sometimes requests were indeed rejected, and when that happened the person rejecting it usually died in three days. I was unable to find someone who reported, first-hand, one such death happening in their own family, but stories such as these evidence that people, particularly in small villages, today still believe in the *Almas Penadas*, and that is certainly one of the main reasons why people, even in big cities, avoid going to places associated with death, such as cemeteries, after nightfall.

4. *Almajona* and *Alamão*
Translation: "Almazon" and "Alamão"

These beings essentially appear to have been an adaptation of the main elements of the Greek Myth of the Amazons. Very little is now known about them, but at one point in the past their Portuguese name was a synonym of "well-fed", perhaps given the fact they were allegedly presented in local stories as very big and fat. Besides, in their feminine form
they also had very big breasts – they used to carry babies on their backs and pull their breasts to the back, in order to feed children while in such infrequent positions. It also deserves to be noted that their husbands were sometimes known as *Alamões* and they were very tall, but the origin of their name is unknown.

---

9   Regrettably, I have long forgotten what the original request was, but it was undoubtedly a weighted product they could get without much effort and which was always almost readily to them.

5. *Balborinho*
Translation: "Hubhub"
Also Known As: *Burburinho, Rosemunho*

This kind of *Alma Penada* appears to have originally been a man who moved the limits of a terrain he owned (which was indeed a very common reason for curses in the myths of Portugal). After he died he became a sort of demon of whirlwinds, causing trouble to people who crossed his paths, often near crossroads. In order to get rid of such a creature you had to throw a razor inside of it, or perhaps utter some kind of popular prayer, both of which would quickly make it vanish.

6. *Basilisco*
Translation: Basilisk

The Basilisk is undoubtedly not a creature native to the myths and legends of Portugal, but one dating back to the Classical Antiquity. Its counterpart from this country has some elements exclusive to it that deserve to be presented. Here, a rooster was said lay an egg once every seven years. When such an uncommon egg was hatched, this lizard-like being was born, and it could kill people just by looking at them. However, if the rooster's owner was able to quickly glance at the beast as soon as it was born, he would quickly kill it, apparently by pure magic, preventing this creature from ever causing any harm to anyone else.

7. *Bicha de Sete Cabeças*
Translation: "Female Monster With Seven Heads"

This strange creature, likely derived from the Laernean Hydra of Greek Mythology, is not precisely a real mythological being from Portugal, and I was even unable to find any reports of people claiming to have ever seen one. Instead, it is mentioned in many local fictional stories as a powerful monster which feeds exclusively on human beings. Invariably, the hero of the story ends up defeating and killing it, then cutting all of its (seven) tongues and preserving them to later prove that it was really him, and nobody else, who killed the fearsome beast.

The main reason for its inclusion here is the fact that this creature is still frequently alluded to nowadays, a *"bicho de sete cabeças"* generally being a metaphor for a problem that seems specially difficult to solve.

8. *Bicho do Cidrão*
Translation: "Strange Animal from *Cidrão*"

Native to *Cidrão*, an area in the island of *Madeira*, the creature known under this name was originally a human shepherd. One day he lost his favorite dog, and in complete desperation uttered words presenting a tacit proposal to the Devil, in which he offered to trade his own soul for the lost canine. The animal soon returned, but when the man died he ended up becoming this strange creature. About it, it is just known that his cries, which sound just like a lamb's voice, presage rain – however, it seems that people haven't heard them in quite some time!

9. *Bruxa* and *Feiticeira*
Translation: Witch and Sorceress

Among the mythological beings presented in this book, the two considered in this chapter are undoubtedly the most famous ones in Portugal nowadays. In fact, it is even fairly common for people to say they do not believe in any of them, that they're just pure fantasy and nothing else, but then add to it a phrase, supposedly coming from Spain, which states *"não acredito em bruxas, mas que as há, há"*, i.e. essentially "I do not believe in witches, but they exist". Also, even in the area of major cities, such as Lisbon, people are still occasionally told not to say so-and-so to a particular person, since that person is a witch – and this is presented as a real fact – and such information could lead her to put some kind of spell in the person alluded to. And so, the local belief in witches is similar to the one in other countries of Europe (e.g. they are accompanied by frogs or black cats), with some elements that seem to be exclusive to this country, and those are the ones mentioned below.

For example, it was once alleged that when a couple had seven daughters in a row, i.e. without any kind of male offspring in between, the seventh would always turn into a witch unless some special requirements took place. What they were appear to have varied widely, but the most common ones were that the oldest sister should be made a godmother to youngest, and that the baby would have to be named *Eva*, *Maria*, or some other significant sacred name derived from the Bible.

Children were the special target of these beings, mostly because they wanted to suck the blood, for a wide

variety of supposed purposes. And so, babies, specially the
unbaptized ones, could be protected from witches by
enrolling the help of people named *Maria* and *Manuel*. Holy
water could be spread around the house to prevent their
entrance (which is a bit strange if you consider that local
tradition also states that these magical women could be
invisible and enter houses through keyholes). Another way
to keep them away was to sleep with an open scissors, in the
form of a cross, under the pillow.

Perhaps the most notable element is the way in which
authors tried to distinguish between sorceresses and witches.
The former could cast the famous evil eye, they never lost
their human form, needed external power to perform their
misdeeds, and a potential joke even claims they were able to
cross the entire ocean, towards Brazil, in a single night while
boarding an eggshell. Then, after a certain number of years
in the evil arts, they would turn into witches and make a
blood pact with the Devil, gaining all sorts of new powers,
the most alluded to being invisibility, the ability to turn into
all kinds of different animals, and being allowed to cast
magic on their own, without requiring constant help from
demonic entities.

Although many other things were said about witches
and sorceresses across the centuries, very notably in the files
of the Portuguese Inquisition, to conclude this chapter there
is an element which undoubtedly has to be stressed – today,
it is still claimed that all people who perform witchcraft must
own at least one copy of the Book of Saint Cyprian[10]. And,

---

10 This is indeed a real book that can still be purchased in local bookstores,
both in Portugal and in Brazil. However, it should be noted it has many
different editions, each one claiming to be the real one and arguing that the
remaining ones are just fake copies with no real power at all.

in fact, when – about 50 years ago – the young son of a woman from *Estoril* was sick, she took him to a local witch, and quickly recognized her as a "real one" based on the fact she did own the aforementioned book – and later, the witch even requested daily goods in return for her services (such as olive oil and a chicken), instead of money, an action which even further proved her credentials to the worried mother, as many years later she ended up telling me!

10. *Cavalo do Pensamento* and *Cavalo do Vento*
Translation: "Horse of Thought" and "Horse of Wind"

Like the *Bicha de Sete Cabeças*, nobody claims to have ever seen these two creatures, but they deserve to be noted here given what is, at the very least, an unusual coincidence. So, in some traditional stories from Portugal, a hero is about to travel and he is requested to pick between the *Cavalo do Pensamento* and the *Cavalo do Vento*. He invariably picks the first, the faster one, which moves as quickly as human thought, but the second, the so-called "horse of wind", may be a veiled allusion to a very old myth, dating back from the Classical Antiquity, according to which mares from a specific area in Portugal – possibly near some mountains close to *Lisboa* – got pregnant by the winds and later gave birth to extremely quick horses. Whether such a reading was actually intended by those who first told those tales, or this is just a pure coincidence and nothing else, will always remain unknown.

11. *Cavalum*
Translation: "Cavalum"

Most legends known in Portugal tend to have somewhat vague limits, in the sense they are supposed to have taken place at some undetermined point in the past. However, the legend of the *Cavalum* is perhaps noteworthy for a very precise location and date associated to it – the island of *Madeira* on the 9th of October of 1803.

According to completely real facts, on that day the island suffered one of the biggest floods in its history[11]; but late legends add to it that it was all caused by the *Cavalum*, a fierce dark horse with bat wings and the uncommon ability to spit fire. This strange being tried to destroy the whole island, to the point he even tore down an old church and threw an image of Jesus Christ into the ocean, in his clear attempt to challenge the power of God. When the deity finally got tired of all the trouble this monster was causing, he captured it and imprisoned it in the caves that still go by the name of *Furnas do Cavalum*. Today, people still seem to hear this creature inside, particularly during storms, still as furious as he was over two centuries ago. As for the image of Christ, it was later recovered back from the surrounding waters, and can still be seen in one of the local churches.

---

11 As of January 2023, it seems to have been the second biggest one in its history.

12. *Cobra Encantada*
Translation: "Enchanted Snake"

This being could apparently be found near the area of *Serpa*, perhaps specifically in the Night of Saint John's (23rd of June). It was a snake with beautiful eyes and really pretty hair, an enchanted version of a woman originally called *Ana*. In order to disenchant her, at first one simply had to call her; she would transform into a powerful bull, then into a black dog, and finally return to the original cursed form of a snake. When that happened, if the person then allowed this snake to give them a kiss, they would apparently die but Ana's spell would finally end[12].

Perhaps she was never disenchanted at all, but the edition of the magazine *A Tradição* which reports this legend also contains the real story of a young woman who was aware of this tradition and appears to have tried to save this ill-fated being. Unfortunately, she ended up fainting when a real snake approached her, perhaps while imaging it was the magical one the legend spoke of.

13. *Coca*
Translation: "Coca"
Also Known As: *Coco, Papão, Sarronca*, and many others…

The *Coca* went under many different names, some male and others female, but it was essentially a creature

---

12 These same elements are also frequent in some legends of the *Mouras Encantadas*. This one features some notable distinctions, such as the fact the snake seems to offer no real rewards for being disenchanted, and so it is unknown if there is any real relationship between those plots, or if the parallelisms evidenced here are just a pure coincidence.

which was used to scare children during the night, likely with the intention of making them fall asleep faster or sleep more when they woke up. Although little is now known about her – to describe her would essentially be the same as trying to portray the anglophone "Boogeyman" – two facts seem to subsist. She covered her entire face with a hood, and so only her shinning red eyes could be seen by people[13]. And also, the expression *"estar à coca"* is still used in Portuguese to describe an action in which you can see something without being seen yourself, certainly as this creature used to do.

There is another being with this same name in the area of *Monção*, once known as *Santa Coca*, but given the fact its celebration – on the 15th of June – presents a reenactment of the battle between Saint George and the dragon, one can easily realize that is just a local name given to the saint's serpentine opponent. And, finally, there is a third *Coca* in Brazil, which was constructed out of elements of these previous two, but her story, which is still famous today in that other country, goes beyond the scope of this work.

14. *Dama Pé de Cabra*
Translation: "Goat Footed Lady"

The story of the two Goat Footed Ladies is still known today and was already retold in my previous work, *Famous Legends From Portugal*, but an additional note deserves to be presented here. According to some local traditions, and as will be further seen in the next section, the

---

13 She may have acquired her name due to the fact that, looking like that she would resemble the "eyes" of a coconut.

Devil – and likely the *Diaba*, his female companion – has the ability to change its shape, but is ultimately unable to change the look of his famous goat feet. That makes it almost certain that these creatures were originally transformations of God's opposer, or one of his many demons, instead of simply women who, for some unknown reason, were born with a very unusual pair of feet.

15. *Diabo* and *Diaba*
Translation: "Devil" and "Female Devil"
Also Known As: *Mafarrico*, *Pedro Malasartes*, *Provinco*, among other almost-endless names…

The Devil is, as you can easily suppose, God's famous opposer, and he is represented as such. He features in a significant number of legends from Portugal, to the point it would be very hard to describe them all in a single book, and so it should be noted that what is important here is not all the stories associated with him, but how he is portrayed in Portugal as a mythological entity. And, in that context, his most notable feature is that he is perfectly willing to help people, to the point it is claimed he made multiple bridges for them, but always expects something in return, usually some drops of blood or the person's soul (as already seen in the case of the *Bicho do Cidrão*). Unexpectedly, after performing his side of the bargain he is also frequently tricked and ends up leaving with no reward at all.

Among his notable features one can find the idea that he can turn into all kinds of animals – and, supposedly, even into humans beings – but always retains the goat imperfection of his feet, perhaps as a way to constantly separate him from the perfection of God's creations. Another of his traditional limitations is that he can know everything else with the exception of people's future. And he is even occasionally given a female companion, the *Diaba*, either his own mother or wife, who has nails similar to a dog's.

But the most curious aspect of this mythological being is how human he is represented as. He is almost always flawed, not a divine-like being at all, and never as powerful as God himself. This is an idea which remains almost until this very day. An 85 year old woman once told me that when she was young her grandmother advised her against going to any dances, telling her that the *Diabo* was always there, dancing together with people. She never went there herself, and never saw him with her own eyes, but one day asked me if this being was real or not, to which I had to answer "who knows!", certainly not wanting to dispel what she had been told across the years.

16. *Duende* and *Anão*
Translation: "Leprechaun" and Dwarf

These two creatures don't really feature significantly in any of the bibliographical information I consulted, perhaps because they were much older than the XIX century and so their original roles may have been replaced by other creatures across time (such as the *Fradinho da Mão Furada* or the *Trasgo*), but I always heard the first one described as a homely being who causes small nuisances and the unexpected noises we all hear in our houses during the night. As for the second entity, local traditions said he lived in a secret place where everything is as small as he is, and that a young child could end up as one of them if someone passed over them in a crib.

17. *Encantado*
Translation: "Enchanted"
Also Known As: *Entreaberto*

Native to the island of *São Miguel*, in the Azores, this being appeared to people around midday and proposed to reveal the location of local treasures. Although this could seem like an extremely nice thing to do, it was actually a dreadful trick – he would later tell people where to dig for the said treasure and kill them from the back while they were doing so, with the only possible way to escape this nefarious subterfuge being the one of also urging him to dig for the treasure, instead of doing it yourself.

18. *Fada*
Translation: Fairy

In Portugal, fairies are usually characters that only appear in storybooks. Perhaps their original, real life, roles were taken over by other mythological beings, such as our once-famous *Mouras Encantadas*, but this purely literary existence is very consistent with how they are portrayed in the rest of Europe. To note just two elements that may differentiate them in local culture, perhaps it can be stressed that these beings can be both good and evil, and that in order to perform their magic tasks they would usually use a "*varinha de condão*", i.e. a magic wand, which was the real source of their powers.

19. *Fradinho da Mão Furada*
Translation: "Little Friar with a Pierced Hand"
Also Known As: *Diabinho da Mão Furada, Pesadelo, Insonho*

Another local being presented in some stories. He was possibly rich, but also as much of a giver as he was a trickster, and he wore a red cap. His pierced hand would seem a very uncommon element, and one specially difficult to explain, if it wasn't for the fact that some of his alternative designations have characteristics that make it possible to explain it – under the name of *Pesadelo*, i.e. "Nightmare", it was believed this being would lie on top of people while they were sleeping and caused their nightmares. He would also try to kill them by covering the person's mouth with his hand, but due to the fact it is pierced, people always ended up surviving his evil attempts.

20. Galgo Negro
Translation: "Black Greyhound"

Black Greyhounds were frequently associated with dark magic in Portugal, and a small legend I came across may partially explain the reason behind it. According to this story, there was once a woman who used to give all the food destined to the poor to domestic animals. When she died, she was punished by reincarnating as this being, a dog forced to eat eternally in the same way of the animals she once fed. There are other versions of this story, including one with a man as a protagonist, but overall it seems that becoming this creature was a sort of penalty.

21. Gambozino
Translation: "Gambozino"
Also Known As: *Piopardo*

A completely fictional animal, which does not even have any kind of real mythology behind it. Instead, the so-called *"caça aos gambozinos"*, i.e. "hunt for *gambozinos*", which is an expression still used in Portugal today, is something that you invite other people to do as a mere joke, since finding these beings is completely impossible and only very silly people would ever believe in their existence.

22. *Gigante*
Translation: Giant

Although there are many creatures similar to giants in Portuguese Mythology, such as the *Olharapo*, under this specific name they are mostly literary beings, which people used to read about in tales of chivalry from the Middle Ages. There, they are represented as all across Europe, i.e. as big human beings with prodigious strength.

23. *Hirã*
Translation: "Hiran"

Likely imported from another country, such as Cape Verde, this creature would be born when a woman had seven consecutive daughters. The seventh would be born with a larger head, and when she turned 12 years old she would then become a serpent and go to live in the sea. Although this description has some elements in common with the ones of the *Bruxa* and the *Lobisomem*, among others, it should be realized that in this specific case there appears to have been no cure to this strange condition, or at least none preserved in literature.

24. *Homem das Sete Dentaduras*
Translation: "Man of the Seven Dentures"

Although the name of this mythological being is very intriguing, chances are that we will never know much about him. He supposedly appeared in the area of *Cerro Vermelho*, in the *Algarve*, always around midday, and devoured people he could find at the time (or perhaps even everything he came across). One can certainly suppose that is why he needed so many dentures – trying to eat a stone or a tree definitely can't be easy… – but that is a mere supposition, since literary sources say nothing else about him and he appears to be long forgotten even among locals of that area.

25. *Homem do Chapéu de Ferro*
Translation: "Man of the Iron Hat"

Certainly as intriguing as the previous one, but at least a little bit more is known about him. According to tradition, the *Homem do Chapéu de Ferro* may have been one of the men who tortured Jesus Christ, and so he was eventually fated to roam the world for all eternity. For unknown reasons he later got an iron hat, one which covered most of his head. He also had a ripped mouth, could spit fire, his skin was the color of bronze, and when he showed up, always in the middle of the night, it was for robbing and killing the people he could find. If this whole thing is still not intriguing enough for you, he was always accompanied by one of three animals – a black pig, a deer with giant horns, and a rooster as black as the darkest night, possibly transformations of the Devil – which seemed to change every night (or every three nights), and when they irritated him, which they invariably ended up doing, very bad things would happen, which directly depended on the current companion by his side. Finally, for unknown reasons he may have been an enemy of the *Velha da Égua Branca*, which may give us the idea that he was also a being local to the area of *Estombar*, in the south of Portugal.

26. *Homem do Saco*
Translation: Bag Man

Seemingly not a being exclusive from Portugal, which also existed in other countries, this man constantly carried a bag, with which he would capture and take away misbehaving children, or only their souls (temporarily) as they prepared to sleep. Perhaps he is somehow related to the *Coca*, another figure used to scare younger people.

27. *Homem na Lua*
Translation: Man on the Moon

Another story which was told to me by an 85 year old, who in turn heard it from her own grandmother (but which is also well attested in multiple literary sources), is the one of a man who had no fear of working on Sundays[14]. Once, he was caught by God cutting brambles on that specific day, and so, as a direct punishment, he was placed on the Moon for all eternity, where he would have to constantly cut his "beloved" brambles, and that is what you can still today see in the darkened sections of Earth's natural satellite.

28. *Homens e Mulheres de Virtude*
Translation: "Virtuous Men and Women"
Also Known As: *Bentos* and *Bentas*

This class of people of either gender were supposed to have significant magical powers, which they frequently used to heal those in need. The easiest way to recognize them was due to the fact they already talked – or cried – while still inside their mother's belly, a strange occurrence which was seen as prophesying their future.

29. *Jãs*
Translation: "Jans"

These invisible beings, potentially related to the fairies of European folklore, sometimes lived in people's houses. When that happened, if someone left some linen inside the house and also placed a cake on top of the table, they would magically weave all the linen during the night. But, if it was simply left there, without any kind of cake as a reward, they would simply burn it all.

---

14 For context, it should be noted that in Portugal traditionally nobody worked on Sundays, instead reserving that day to attend mass, have lunch with their family, and rest.

30. *João Pestana*
Translation: Sandman
Also Known As: *Chosco, Pedro-Chosco*

An entity which made children asleep by putting some grains of sand in their eyes. There seem to have been some songs that people could sing to counteract the effect of his powers. Interestingly, the few examples of literature which mention him make it sound like he was still very famous in the beginning of the XX century. Today, it seems his name is just barely known as a mere metaphor for sleep, with no specific tales associated with it.

31. *Lagarto da Penha de França*
Translation: "Lizard of *Penha de França*"

This creature deserves to be noted here due to the fact it is one of the few legendary creatures directly associated with the city of Lisbon. According to its legend, at some point before the year of 1755 a man fell asleep near a tree in an area of this city still known today as *Penha de França*. A snake approached him, and was in fact about to attack him, when the Virgin Mary intervened and miraculously caused a big lizard to appear, which scared away the deadly snake and saved this man from a potential death. The story is still widely known in the area, some intriguing tiles representing the episode can be seen there too, and inside the local church you can even spot multiple allusions to it.

32. *Larouco*
Translation: "Larouco"
Also Known As: *Larauco*

In the very north of Portugal you can find a mountain known as *Serra do Larouco*. It was seemingly named as such because *Larauco*, a god or mythological being of the Ancient Celts, once lived there. Nothing else is now known about it.

33. *Lobisomem*
Translation: Werewolf
Also Known As: *Blisome, Corredor, Corrilário, Zargão*

Along with the *Bruxas* and the *Almas Penadas*, this was clearly among the most famous mythological beings of Portugal. However, even if you're familiar with werewolves from other world traditions, the ones associated with them in this country are quite unique, and there's even a very extensive literature about them and how they were portrayed in different areas of Portugal. Their main ideas are briefly presented here.

Supposedly, a *Lobisomem* could only be created in one of three ways – through witchcraft (a *Bruxa* had to say some words to implant this curse); through an illicit sexual relationship, such as one between a godfather and a niece; or when a woman had seven consecutive children of the male gender. The first path could be dispelled through many different ways. If a woman was already expecting this to be her seventh male child, she could give him a sacred name, such as *Adão* or *Bento*, and make her oldest son the godfather to his youngest. Also, the person affected could later *"correr fado"*[15], which required him to perform some tasks, at the end of which he would need to be stricken in a very particular way and specific place of his body – and if performed correctly, he would then stop being affected by this curse!

But what did this kind of *Lobisomem* really do, if he wasn't that similar to other international creatures of the same name? Strangely enough, in most versions he is essentially a harmless creature, which on Wednesdays and Fridays – or other days of the week, depending on oral traditions which changed from one village to another – would leave his house during the night to run through seven villages, churches, bridges, etc. He would remove his clothes somewhere and then would start running, soon turning into an animal – not just specifically a wolf, but also a donkey (sometimes called a *Blisome*), pig, dog (the *Corrilário*, which was also a kind of *alma penada*), cat, chicken, horse (the *Zargão*), or even a *Pato Marreco* – usually until he heard a rooster crowing, someone managed to draw his blood, or his fated time finally arrived.

Overall, the Portuguese werewolf was not a very scary creature, but it was mostly a nuisance and a strange kind of curse that some people faced in their lives. Although nowadays this native form of the creature appears to be increasingly forgotten and replaced by the anglophone version (where they are created by being bitten by a wolf, transform during the full moon, etc.), some people are still aware of the original local forms. An 85 year old once told me she had had a friend whose husband was a *Lobisomem*;

---

15 This expression is hard to translate because even in its native language it appears to make little sense. Translated literally, it means "run fate", possibly in the sense of accomplishing what is destined to him.

whenever he wanted to go out at night and his wife tried to prevent him from doing so, he would fall to the floor and have massive (epileptic?) fits. Unfortunately those two people are long dead, and so I could not obtain more information about such episodes from them, but such information appears to prove that belief in these creatures, under their native form, was still alive and well at the end of the XX century.

34. *Luz da Caniceira*
Translation: Light from *Caniceira*

Naturally associated with a village that goes by the name of *Caniceira*, this creature could be simply defined as a very mysterious light that people often spotted during the night. There seem to be multiple legends for its origin, but the most common one states that this is the soul of a young woman who died inside of an old traditional oven, into which she was somehow put by a family member who was angry at her.

35. *Mão de Ferro*
Translation: Iron Hand

This entity is among the strangest ones of Portuguese Mythology. Not much appears to have ever been explained about it, but this was an invisible being which gave people powerful slaps, often at seemingly random times and places. Perhaps it was a strange manifestation of the *Diabo*, perhaps it derived from some chivalry romance of the Middle Ages, but an even stranger piece of information adds that one such being once taught at the University of Salamanca (likely in the strange *Cova de Salamanca*, where the Devil was once believed to teach his acolytes).

36. *Maria Gancha, Maria da Grade* and *Maria da Manta*
Translation: "Mary Hook", "Mary of the Grid" and "Mary of the Blanket"

Another being used to scare children, the *Maria Gancha* lived at the bottom of wells and would supposedly grab the young fellows who carelessly played around those places, killing them by drowning. By parallelism, and although I was not able to find much rock-solid information about her two other counterparts, it is safe to assume they were also entities used for similar tasks – the first likely carrying a grid, had big beautiful eyes and long hair, the second a blanket of some sort – *Maria* being a very popular name in Portugal which, to this very day, is still used as the general name for unknown women.

37. *Maria Marcela*
Translation: "Mary Marcela"

Otherwise unknown, *Maria Marcela* was believed to be a woman who once possessed a very large golden staff. When she died, her staff was somehow hidden somewhere near a road and was then completely forgotten. None of this would ever be very worthy of note if it wasn't for the fact that, according to local tradition, whoever obtains it will soon rule all over Portugal and Spain. So, in case you want to start looking for it right away, it can perhaps be revealed this story was collected near the village of *Cinfães*, but since little else is known about any of it, the legendary staff can be hidden literally anywhere.

38. *Maria Molha* and *Maria das Pernas Compridas*
Translation: "Mary Wet" and "Mary of the Long Legs"

In this other case, the entity alluded to appears to be nothing else besides a simple metaphor for rain. Her names were given because rain naturally gets people wet, while she was supposed to have some "long legs" since, from a symbolic standpoint, they indeed come all the way from the sky up the ground.

39. *Marinha*
Translation: Mermaid
Also Known As: *Sereia*

An important note deserves to begin this specific entry – although I previously retold the legend of one *Dona Marinha* in my *Famous Legends From Portugal*, nothing in that story makes it clear that she was ever a mermaid. She apparently had lived in the ocean, and was initially unable to talk, but even in the original literary sources nothing ever stated she was indeed a half-fish being, and the content of the plot in itself even seems to indicate otherwise, since she later lives on land. In fact, she apparently was named "*Marinha*", i.e. "marine", exclusively over the fact she came from the sea.

But then, for some reason, across the centuries *Marinha* started to become the native word for what was later called a *Sereia*, a half-woman being who was a fish from her waist down (male counterparts are rare in Portuguese culture, perhaps with the exclusion of the *Tritão*). They seem to have come, originally, from Greek Mythology, but they also have some elements which appear to be entirely native to Portugal. First, they were not always born with this strange shape, with some legends of varying content mentioning they were originally women who ended up suffering some kind of sea-related curse. Then, readers are presented with the idea they frequently sung by the local beaches, doing so as perfectly as the angels in heaven do (i.e. very beautifully), and that they infrequently combed their beautiful hair around beaches. These elements seem to prove that, locally, these creatures did live in the sea but could be found in land too.

Nowadays, the word *Sereia* has almost entirely substituted the old *Marinha* – in the city of *Porto*, for example, you can find a XVIII century palace named the *Palácio das Sereias* over the fact it features, at the entrance, two of these beings holding columns, but by the time it was built it seems the old word was already rarer than the new one.

40. *Medo*
Translation: Fear
Also Known As: *Coisa Ruim, Trango-Mango*

It is possible that these beings are a special form of *Almas Penadas*, with potential descriptions and names varying a lot, e.g. some people used to say they appear at midday, while others reserved their presence for midnight alone. Overall, they seem to have been a personification of everything that is scary, and often presented themselves to people in groups, where the plural *Medos* was used for them instead.

An old lady from *Estoril* once shared with me a story possibly related to this entity. There was, when she was younger, a local house in which nobody was ever seen. For some reason, she and other local children started to think this was the *Casa do Medo*, the house where Fear itself lives, and so they had the habit of going there and calling for the inhabitant to come outside – and yet, nobody ever got out of the house or replied back to them. I tried to gather more information on this entity from her, but she always insisted that *Medo* was Fear and that it lived in that house, without ever knowing anything else about it. Since her grandparents were from the north of Portugal, chances are that she may have been told stories of the *Medos* when she was young, but never paid much attention to them and they are now completely lost. The house still remains in its original place and, strangely enough, to this very day nobody can ever be seen living inside of it.

41. *Meigas*
Translation: "Gentle Ones"

Little is known about these creatures, with the exception that they lived by rivers and dressed in white. Maybe they were entities associated with water in some areas of the north of Portugal.

42. *Menino dos Olhos Grandes*
Translation: "Little Boy with Big Eyes"

Native to *Olhão*, in the *Algarve*, this being appears to have been so famous locally that a statue representing him was eventually erected in the city, where it can still be seen today. Essentially, its legend states that a few decades ago a young boy with big eyes could frequently be spotted in the city, always during the night. He would occasionally cry, other times he would carry a small basket with unknown content, but he was always super heavy and never said a single word to anyone. One day, as mysteriously as when he first appeared, he vanished and was never seen again by anyone – and yet, there are still some people alive today who claim to have seen him with their own eyes!

43. *Moura Encantada*[16]
Translation: "Enchanted Moorish Woman"

Out of the legendary beings from Portuguese Mythology, the *Moura Encantada* was once likely the most popular and famous one, but unfortunately its popularity has been rapidly dropping in the last century, to the point I was ultimately unable to find anyone who still believed in them, and very few people who still knew what they are – and, in this case, they always insisted that such a thing was only a fantasy and nothing else.

Overall, these entities could be found in fountains and hard to access places, such as cliffs, caverns, ruined ancient buildings and *antas*. They would talk to people, frequently in

---

16 Although these beings can also be male and children, their most famous form is female.

the Night of Saint John's (23rd of June), and propose some kind of task which, if performed correctly, would greatly reward the person and finally remove the enchantment of the Moorish Woman. Invariably, through their enormous curiosity or greed, people would fail the task, an action which doubled the original enchantment (although it is unclear what that consisted of). Other versions presented them as shape-shifting snakes, sometimes with pretty hair, and when people failed to answer a question correctly, or just refused to kiss the slippery animal, their curse would remain unchanged.

There are many legends associated with the *Mouras Encantadas* preserved in books from Portugal, but they are apparently no longer told in oral forms, except in events specially designed to ensure these stories are not completely lost. Although I still heard some of them when I was younger, it should be stressed, once again, that people don't believe in them any more, and so they appear to be progressively forgotten.

44. *Mula Fantasma*
Translation: Phantom Mule

In the area of *Sintra* you may be able to find a small river known as *Rio da Mula*, next to which there is a small dam. According to a very short story collected on location, the place was named so because, during the night, sometimes a mule could be heard there, but nobody was ever be able to spot her, and so people started to believe it was some kind of ghost animal. Out of sheer curiosity, I decided to visit the place myself and try to hear it, but I was ultimately never able to.

45. *Olharapo*, *Olharapa* and *Olhapim*
Translation: "Olharapo", "Olharapa" and "Olhapim"

These three entities are clearly related, and their name directly alludes to the fact they probably had an unusual number of eyes, but how each of them looked like seems to vary from one literary source to another. The *Olharapo* and the *Olharapa* were husband and wife, and in the very limited number of stories which reached us it is claimed they both had a single eye in the middle of their forehead. But, eventually confused with the *Olhapim*, it is also stated that these species may have had one eye, three (two in the front, one in the back of the head), or even four. Their stories are almost entirely lost – I've read two about the first species, but none concerning the *Olhapins* – but the most notable one seems to present the *Olharapo* as a one-eyed giant in a plot similar to the one of Polyphemus from Homer's *Odyssey*. Perhaps this was once the local and native name for the Cyclops? Given the limited number of stories which reached us, it is impossible to conclude anything about such a question.

46. *Peeira dos Lobos*
Translation: "She Who Stands Next to Wolves"
Also Known As: *Lobeira*

If a *Lobisomem* was traditionally born when a woman had seven male children in a row, some traditions – likely from the north of Portugal, where wolves were commonly seen – stated that when she had seven female ones a *Peeira de Lobos* could be born. This woman, as she grew older, would be fated to move into the mountains and live with wolves for seven years, or at least until her curse was lifted if her blood was drawn. What she would do together with the wolves is mostly unknown, but they seemingly lived in a group and she may have had the ability to talk to them, perhaps as if she was shepherding these animals.

47. *Porca de Murça*
Translation: Pig from *Murça*

If you are ever in the area of *Murça*, in its main square you may be able to spot an ancient statue of a being that popularly goes under this name. According to the legend, it is the representation of a gigantic pig which once lived in this area, but which the local population eventually united against and ended up killing. But, whether the statue really represents a pig, or a completely different animal (such as a bear), is still completely up for debate.

48. *Pretinho do Barrete Encarnado*
Translation: "Little Black Guy with Red Cap"

This little black guy, who always wore a red cap, may have been a young son of the Devil, who against his father's wishes was good – and sometimes, evil – to other children. Although little else is known about him, one definitely has to consider it may have some kind of relationship with the *Saci* from Brazil, who is also represented in a very similar way.

49. *Secular das Nuvens*
Translation: "Secular of the Clouds"

Among the stories from Portuguese Mythology, this is arguably one of the most violent ones. It claims that if a man was killed in a way that slowly but completely destroyed his body from the toes to the head, and then all his remains – including the blood and grinded bones – were safely stored for an entire year, his soul would then ascend into the heavens and he would become a *Secular das Nuvens*, who would live for 100 years (hence its name) and was able to cause and control storms. Although unexpectedly strange, this legend was perhaps derived from an even older local belief in the idea that excommunicated men could be seen among the clouds.

50. *Tágides*
Translation: Nymphs of the Tagus River

Although they are not purely mythological beings, the *Tágides* deserve to be briefly noted here since they are specially known from the *Lusíadas*, the epic poem of *Luís de Camões*. There, when initially seeking his inspiration, the poet asks for the help of these beings, the nymphs of his local Tagus River. Although the whole idea was based on the Nymphs of Classical Mythology, who also inhabited similar locations, their local name appears to have first been used in the XVI century, and through the famous epic ended up reaching us, but nobody seems to consider them as anything else but poetic figures.

51. *Tardo*[17]
Translation: "Tardo"

The information about this creature tends to be very unreliable, vague and uncertain, with some people even considering it just as an alternate name for the *Lobisomem* or a transformation of the Devil. Some used to say he lived only during the night, was a trickster and able to speak with a human voice. Others stated he was as small as a puppy or a cat, and when he peed on people they would invariably be late for their appointments – potentially an origin for his name, as in the expression "*chegar tarde por causa do Tardo*", i.e. "being late because of the Lat-o". Other people mentioned he owned a red cap which, if ever taken away from him, would magically enrich the person who managed to accomplish such a deed.

In any case, the multiplicity of very different elements attributed to this same being appear to indicate his name was once famous all over Portugal, but each area may have associated different characteristics to him, which can potentially explain why it is almost impossible to establish a horizontal and stable portrait for this being.

52. *Tatro Azeiteiro*
Translation: "Olive Oil Worker Tatro"

Perhaps another transformation of the Devil, that entity so frequent in stories from Portugal, this one was a

---

17 According to some authors, the *Tardo*, the *Tatro* and the *Trasgo* could potentially be different transformations of the Devil, their similar name being derived from Tartarus, the deepest part of the underworld in Greek and Roman Mythology.

personification of fog. Seemingly, he produced olive oil, or just the smell of it, whenever fog appeared, but women could keep it away by moving a certain part of their looms during the night. These ideas suggest that, originally, he may have had a more complex mythology surrounding him, but the information currently available makes it impossible to know much more about what it could have been.

53. *Teresa Fidalgo*
Translation: Teresa Fidalgo

This ghost deserves to be presented here, most of all, to make it clear that it is a completely fake one. According to the supposed story, a young lady named *Teresa Fidalgo* lived near the area of *Sintra*. One day, back in 1983, as she was traveling around the area she suffered a deadly car crash, and now she haunts the exact place where she died, causing others to suffer car crashes too. You may even have seen such a video online, but in case it is not perfectly obvious yet, the whole story – and the video, too – are completely fake, and there is no credibly established information about this potential ghost, which is not even a locally famous myth, before the release of the now infamous video.

54. *Trasgo*
Translation: "Trasgo"

Yet another potential transformation of the Devil, some say related to fogs, which the literary sources state could be kept away by ringing church bells. In what seems to be a different version of this creature, he was alleged to live in people's houses and occasionally cause some minor nuisances, such as playing pranks on women while they slept. Curiously, he appears to have had other sub-types, such as the *Trasgo Loiceiro*, which apparently moved around benches and tableware in general.

55. *Tritão*
Translation: Triton

If you ever come to Portugal and visit the *Palácio da Pena* in *Sintra*, you will there find a place commonly known as the *Pórtico do Tritão*, where this being holds the beautiful window placed over him, as you can see in the cover art for this same book. That creature is actually part of a very old legend associated with Portugal, which even dates all the way back to Classical Antiquity. According to it, in a cavern somewhere near Lisbon this being could, many centuries ago, be heard playing his beautiful music. Unfortunately, the precise location of his once-famous lair is now long lost, but this is perhaps one of the oldest extant legends associated with this country, which may explain the being's notable prominence in this palace.

56. *Velha da Égua Branca*
Translation: "Old Woman of the White Mare"

From the area of *Estombar*, according to the legend this old woman refused to give a piece of bread to Jesus Christ when he was alive. In return, he cursed her to have the next bread she cut turn into pure blood. When this later happened, she got really scared and ended up dying very quickly, but her soul, still facing a divine curse, was condemned to roam the world in a white mare for all eternity, while carrying the same knife she used to cut her bread. She usually does it under the moonlight, but a tantalizing piece of information seemingly states that she was an enemy of the *Homem do Chapéu de Ferro*. Not much else is known about this potential relationship, but it is worth noting that, at the very least, both figures appear to have been cursed by Jesus, given the unchristian way in which they acted towards him.

57. *Zorra de Odelouca*
Translation: "Odelouca's Fox"
Also Known As: *Zorra Berradeira*

A special kind of *Alma Penada*, according to the most famous version of her legend she was once a woman who used to move around the limits of her terrains. After death, her soul was condemned to roam the world, and specially the area where she had once lived, making her strange noises after midnight, which are allegedly so horrifying that they madden or kill the people who hear them.

----- THE END -----

A Final Request – this book is part of an attempt to bring traditional myths and legends from Portugal to English-speaking audiences. If you enjoyed its content please write a review for this book and share it with others. Depending on people's feedback, I may write other books about these

subjects in the future, but that is entirely up to readers like
YOU. Your feedback truly matters!

Printed in Great Britain
by Amazon

33475015R00027